An Odd Body

Church, Witness, and Culture in 1 and 2 Corinthians

Corinth was a large commercial trade port and included people and beliefs from a diverse area of the Mediterranean. An ancient Greek city, it was destroyed in 146 B.C.E. by the Romans and rebuilt about 100 years later. In the days of the early Christian movement, residents and travelers were interested in and influenced by both Greek and Roman culture and philosophy, including an array of religious beliefs and practices.

The population of Corinth included a considerable number of Jews, like many major cities of the ancient world. When the Apostle Paul visited the city on his mission of preaching the gospel of Jesus, he began with the Jewish believers. The fledgling Christian community in Corinth also included people new to both the teachings of Judaism and of Jesus Christ. They were attempting to define themselves in contrast to a diverse culture. While they struggled with problems and divisions, they sincerely wanted to follow Christ and sought advice from Paul as a trusted leader.

The earliest Christian communities relied on leadership from people like Paul who traveled from place to place teaching and preaching. Continued guidance to the fledgling congregations was offered through written messages. The Christian scriptures include two such letters from Paul to the church at Corinth, though Paul actually wrote a number of letters to the church in Corinth. Not all of these have been preserved. Some scholars suggest that the letter we call Second Corinthians is actually a composite of portions of more than one letter.

First Corinthians was written around year 55 of the Common Era while Paul was in Ephesus. He wrote the letter in response to reports of troubling practices and divisions within the congregation. The Christians in Corinth had also asked for specific counsel on various subjects relating to congregational life and Christian practice.

Second Corinthians was likely written shortly after the first; there is indication it was written by Paul from Macedonia. This letter was a response to false teachers who influenced the church at Corinth. Paul writes to outline his own teaching, to defend his authority and integrity as a leader, and to ask Corinthians to prepare for a visit from him.

Throughout both letters Paul suggests ways in which following Christ and his teachings brings about a transformation in the believers. These believers were committed to following Jesus, but they faced the same struggles as the rest of the world around them. They were confronted with issues regarding personal relationships, business dealings, sexuality, and congregational life. Sometimes they succumbed to the same weaknesses and mistakes as their neighbors. Paul reminds them that they are guided by the good news of Jesus Christ.

ABOUT THE WRITER

Teresa Moser is an ordained minister in the Pacific Northwest Mennonite Conference and lives in Portland, Oregon.

Welcome to Good Ground!

Now that you know a little about the topic for this unit, let us introduce you to Good Ground, the series. Good Ground is a unique approach to Bible study. It lets the Bible ask most of the questions and lets participants struggle with the answers. When we ask, "How can I be saved?" the Bible asks, "Whom will you serve?" When we ask, "What will happen to me when I die?" the Bible asks, "What does the Lord require of you?" When we ask, "Whom does God love best?" the Bible asks, "Who is your neighbor?" Good Ground goes to the Scriptures for questions, not just answers.

Here's how each session is structured and what you can expect:

PART I: PREPARATION

We assume that you want to dig into Bible texts enough to do a little reading and thinking between sessions. In this section you are given the Bible passage(s) for the session, a key verse, a summary of the text and the issues it raises, and a three-page study on the text. The section concludes with "Things to think about," which offers some practical applications for everyday living.

We realize that in an age of prepackaged goods and 15-second sound bites, advance preparation may be a challenge. At the same time, we believe that for God's Word to be relevant to us, we need to do what it takes to ready our hearts and minds.

PART II: SESSION

Here we offer tips for your group when it meets, whether at church, in a home, or in some other setting. Good Ground uses a method for study that begins with everyday life (Focus), moves into an examination of what the Bible says (Engage the Text), then suggests life applications (Respond). The Closing wraps up the study in a brief worship experience.
One of the unique features about Good Ground studies is that they tap into a variety of learning styles. Some people learn best through the traditional lecture and discussion, but many others learn through visuals, imagination, poetry, role-playing, and the like. Through these varied learning experiences, Good Ground gets participants involved in the learning, moving beyond the head and into concrete living from the heart.

PART III: LEADER GUIDELINES

We recognize that in many adult groups today, responsibility for leading is passed around within the group—hence the inclusion of notes for the leader in the participant's book. For these sessions to work best, however, those who lead must be prepared ahead of time. This section outlines what materials will be needed for the session, suggests some resources, and offers some tips for making the session come alive. If you are a regular leader of Good Ground, you will likely be aware of our other teaching/leading resources that orient you to our learning philosophy and methods.

Enjoy working with Good Ground as you journey in your faith, growing to be more like Christ!

Julie Garber, editor
Byron Rempel-Burkholder, editor
Ken Hawkley, adult education consultant

Session 1

The Christian Community: An Alternative Way to Live

PART I: PREPARATION

Bible passage: 1 Corinthians 6:1-11

Key verse: But you were washed, you were sanctified, you were justified in the name of the Lord Jesus Christ and in the Spirit of our God (1 Cor. 6:11).

Summary: Paul discovers that members of a congregation in Corinth have a dispute, probably over property, and have gone to the civil courts to settle their disagreement. He uses their case to emphasize that Christians must die to the old way of doing things, including using the court system, and live fully in the new age. What difference does it make if we claim to be followers of Christ, but live no differently than we lived before becoming Christians? What point is there in claiming to be a community under the authority of the new age and then submitting to authorities from outside? It is, as Paul says, "already a defeat for you" (6:7). In what respect can we say today that we, as Christians, live in a new age? Where must we admit that we are no different from people who live according to the old way? As people of the new age, would we go so far as to put faith ahead of our financial assets? How should we distinguish ourselves from the old age?

Study

Paul's letters to young Christian churches served several purposes. In general, they encouraged and supported young congregations, taught and corrected their theology, and instructed new Christians in the practices of church life and leadership. But Paul's letters also responded to very specific questions or problems that developed in young churches trying to find their way. In Corinth, Paul spoke out when he became aware that members of one of the congregations there were taking other church members to civil courts to settle disputes.

May we all so love each and all
selfish claims deny,
so that each one for the
other will not hesitate to die.
Even so our Lord has loved us,
for your lives he gave his life.
Still he grieves and still he
suffers, for our selfishness
and strife.

—Nicolaus L. von Zinzendorf, 1723

Why did this simple issue matter so much to Paul? He was only dealing with a simple property dispute between church members, not a criminal case that would have been prosecuted by Roman authorities. It's true that the Roman government allowed Jews to handle property disputes according to their own religious teachings. And since Christians were likely given the same rights, being thought of as Jews, the Corinthian congregation could have handled this case themselves. But is Paul angry just about turf?

Not likely. In fact, Paul was the one who said earthly powers and institutions are ordained of God, which includes the church and the Roman government. The problem was deeper than the question of rights and authorities. Paul's purpose in this passage is to remind Christians that while power is established by God, it is corrupted by human beings. The Romans had perverted power for their own interests. Christians had made a commitment, on the other hand, to live a new way. The new way is the way of trust in God and trust in the body of Christ. To resort to civil courts was to betray the new covenant. Moreover, the fracture in the community could not be repaired from without by civil courts. Trust could only be reestablished from within.

Paul chides the congregation for getting outside help for such a small matter. It's like taking a noisy neighbor to the Supreme Court. "If such matters come up, are you going to take them to be settled by people who have no standing in the church? Shame on you! Surely there is at least one wise person in your fellowship who can settle a dispute between fellow Christians" (6:4-5 TEV). Paul continues with his admonishment, saying that for being former sinners, they aren't much different from people of the old age, especially when they defraud and wrong others in their own congregation. Instead they should remember that God claimed them and accepts them and they are different now—as long as they live in Christ.

Trust your neighbor

In verses 7 and 8, Paul makes the shocking suggestion that it would be better among believers to be cheated than to drag another believer into court. In the Christian community, maintaining good relationships is more important than protecting one's assets. Trusting the wisdom of the church community in settling disputes is evidence of the transformation that Paul calls being "justified in the name of the Lord Jesus Christ and in the Spirit of our God" (v. 11). Among those who do not share the bonds of Christian faith, being right or assigning blame may be the order of the day, but within the Christian community, maintaining positive relationships is more important.

I recently heard of two members of a congregation who had a boundary dispute with financial implications. The two men were neighbors and farmers. When their attempts to settle the conflict were not successful, one of the men decided to "drop it." When a third friend pointed out there was clear evidence that would stand up in a court of law, the farmer said he had decided he would rather have the relationship than the money. For the sake of the relationship, he chose to not litigate. Maybe this is what Jesus was talking about when he said "if anyone strikes you on the right cheek, turn the other also; and if anyone wants to sue you and take your coat, give your cloak as well" (Matt. 5:39b-40).

Now there may be occasions when a dispute is truly irreconcilable and the people involved need to let it go. However, a consistent pattern of ignoring conflict often leads to repressed hostility that destroys relationships instead of saving them. Perhaps the two men in the boundary dispute considered doing nothing or going to court to be the only options for resolving their disagreement, but there is a third way. They could have turned to the wise counsel of their church. Maybe some of their fellow church members could have helped these two men consider new ways to look at their problem and identify ways to compromise or work together so that each would benefit from the solution. The Christian community Paul envisions is one in which such alternatives are regularly sought and practiced.

The Christian community struggles today with its identity much as the Corinthians did in the first century. The world pulls in one direction, urging the church to conform to the way things are. The gospel pulls in the opposite direction, demanding that Christians be different, that they live in a new age. Does the fact that we all pay taxes, vote in civil elections, live according to civil law, and enjoy nice cars and houses mean that we have succumbed to the world? Or does our devotion to the church, our work for justice, our stewardship, and trust of our neighbor witness to the priority of the gospel in our lives? Perhaps the answer lies in whether people of the world (or what Paul would call the old age) can tell that we are people of the new age.

Things to think about:
1. Use other people as a mirror to see your reflection. Ask several people outside your congregation how they would know that you are a Christian. Be prepared to share their reflections with the group?
2. Also think about how your congregation handles conflict? What mechanisms, such as mediation or counseling, are set up to handle disputes? How do you think the church would handle, or should handle, disputes that involve property, finances, or child custody?
3. Have a family discussion about whether you think the court system is capable of making decisions as Christians would make them and whether you would use the courts or avoid them today?

PART II: SESSION

Focus (10 MINUTES)

Take time for announcements and sharing, and then choose one of the following options to focus on the topic for this session.

Option A: Decide which one of the following Christian symbols you would wear as jewelry or display on the bumper of your car: a cross, a fish, a cup (connoting the cup of cold water), or bread. Meet for a few minutes with others in the group who chose the same symbol. Talk briefly about what the symbol says about you or your faith that you would like others to know. Let a volunteer from your group summarize your discussion for the large group.

Transition: Paul demands that church members, who have committed themselves to a new life in Christ, live according to the dictates of the "new age," and not according to the ways of the "old age." How would people know today that you are a Christian? Is the only distinguishing mark of your faith a piece of jewelry or a bumpersticker? In 1 Corinthians 6:1-11, Paul says that how we live speaks volumes about who we are.

Option B: Decide as a group what the greatest non-theological dispute is in your denomination or congregation. Is it how the church building will be used? Is it a dispute with a contractor who built the building? or with the nursery school personnel that use the church? Is the denomination struggling over property in other countries, or with state or provincial authorities over schools? Do church people argue over how church money is invested? Whatever it is, discuss for five to ten minutes how you think the church should handle the issue. Should the church take legal action? Why? Is there a way to settle the issue with mediators? How? Should the church avoid civil squabbles by bowing out of conflict? At what point?

Transition: Paul tells a Corinthian congregation that they should avoid settling their disputes in civil courts and live according to the new way of the gospel. Look at 1 Corinthians 6:1-11 and two other texts to see what it means to live according to the "new age."

Engage the Text (20 MINUTES)

Option A: According to both Christian and Hebrew scriptures, conflict within the community of faith is not a new problem. Look up the following passages; read silently and give brief descriptions or read the passages aloud: 1 Samuel 8:4-7 (leadership); 2 Samuel 12:1-15 (murder); Acts 6:1-6 (welfare); 1 Corinthians 3:1-9 (authority). Divide into four groups to discuss the following questions.

1. How did the faith community handle the conflict in the passage?
2. Identify "old age" thinking in the passage?
3. What are the "new age" expectations placed on the people in the passage?
4. Think of a modern parallel to the passage. How would the story play out if the faith community handled it in accordance with the gospel?

Choose a reporter from your group, and return to the large group to summarize your group's discussion. Take time for questions or remarks after each report.

Option B: Listen as volunteers read 1 Corinthians 6:1-6; Matthew 6:1-18; Romans 14:1-12; and 1 Corinthians 9:19-23. Divide into small groups, each group focusing on a different passage. Work together in the small group to determine what the "new age" manner of living is, according to the passage. List your definitions on newsprint and post them for the large group to see. Choose a reporter and return to the large group to hear about the work of the other groups. As a large group, talk about whether any of the definitions contradict one another. Taken all together, can you think of any acts of gospel living missing from the list? What are they?

Respond (15 MINUTES)

Option A: Choose one or more of the following scenarios and apply the principles of new life in Christ to it. How would it come out?

—A couple in the church is divorcing, having fallen out of love after fifteen years of marriage. They have three children in private school, an upscale house, and two nice cars. The wife has not worked since they've been married.

—A teenager in the church was badly hurt in a car accident while riding with another member of the youth group. Her injuries will require several surgeries and her family has poor insurance coverage. Her parents are considering suing the driver to cover their daughter's treatment.

—A woman in the church has inherited $100,000 from an aunt she helped care for. Her first thought is to quickly invest the money in the stock market for her own retirement. Then her alma mater, her church, and a local charity visit her to encourage her to make a sizable contribution out of her inheritance to fund their work.

—A family in the church has several concerns about public schools in their town. Military recruiters visit the high school regularly, offering young people "opportunities of a lifetime." Students must go through metal detectors each morning. A history teacher often campaigns for political candidates in a classroom of seniors who will be able to vote in the next election. The parents are trying to decide whether it is better to let their children stay in public school and be witnesses to another way of living or whether it is better to enroll them in private school as a way of protesting the status quo.

Option B: Show your true colors. On a slip of paper, write down several marks of a Christian that would distinguish a believer from people in general. Gather the slips of paper and compile a list of the marks. Talk together about whether a Christian with these marks could live and operate in the society in general or whether he or she would live apart from society in order to be faithful. Then take turns telling where you are personally in relation to the list of marks you've compiled. What would Paul say to you if he visited your congregation today?

For a variation on this exercise, tear or cut pictures from magazines to make a composite portrait of a Christian living in the "new age." How would a Christian dress? Where would a Christian live? In what kind of house? What kind of work would a "new age" Christian do? In what would a Christian invest time and talents? Display your artwork for the congregation to see.

Closing (5 MINUTES)

Gather in a circle to sing or read the words of "Heart with loving heart united." Take hands and pray silently for the relationship between you and the person on your left and your right. When you have finished your prayer, give that person's hand a gentle squeeze.

PART III: LEADER GUIDELINES

Items Needed

Newsprint or chalkboard
Magazines
Bibles
Pens and scrap paper

Resources

Snyder, Graydon. *First Corinthians: A Faith Community Commentary.*
    Macon, Ga.: Mercer University Press, 1992.

Inhauser, Marcos. *1 Corinthians: the Community Struggles.* Elgin, Ill.:
    Brethren Press, 1994.

Mays, James L., ed. *Harper's Bible Commentary.* San Francisco: Harper
    & Row, 1988.

Tips for Leading

1. Begin each session with time for announcements, offering, and other "housekeeping" chores. This will be the one time each week when the church family can support each other.

2. Study the lesson several days in advance and give some thought to responses for each activity. If discussion lags, offer your responses to keep things moving quickly and smoothly. If conversation flows easily, hold your comments. Let others speak.

3. Think of yourself as a moderator. Urge quiet people to enter into conversation and ask those who talk often to wait until the group has heard from others.

4. Some scenarios in the lesson may hit very close to home. Use care when discussing topics that make participants feel vulnerable. Agree as a group that all comments made in the group are said in confidence. Give people a safe place to talk about their personal lives, but also respect their wishes for privacy.

Session 2

Marriage: A Special Calling

PART I: PREPARATION

Bible passage: 1 Corinthians 7:1-24

Key verse: However that may be, let each of you lead the life that the Lord has assigned, to which God called you (1 Cor. 7:17).

Summary: In chapter 7, Paul uses his three favorite topics, marriage (or gender), race, and slavery, to make a theological statement. At first it looks like Paul is simply giving Christians rules to be married by or single by. But, in general, Paul is teaching Christians more about the new age. The "givens" we are handed in life, he says, are not important in our new life in Christ. No matter how we find completion of ourselves in a marriage partner, our ultimate completeness is in Christ. If we are slaves in this world, we are free in the new age, and if we are free, we are slaves to the gospel. And similarly in the new way ushered in by Jesus, there is neither Jew nor Gentile, only children of God. We cannot change our past, but we can live in the new age according to our calling. What does that mean for us in real terms as spouses, people with passions, people in broken relationships, and people longing to relate to others?

Study

Reading Paul's letters is a little like overhearing one end of a telephone conversation. We only hear the comments of the person in the room with us. We hear responses to unknown questions and comments about unheard things. At the beginning of 1 Corinthians 7, Paul specifically refers to something on which he has been asked to comment. A large part of his speech is a discussion about marriage and remarriage, singleness and divorce, apparently in response to questions from Christians in Corinth.

We know something about the social and religious context of Corinth, out of which these questions arise. The population is estimated to have been nearly three-quarters of a million people at the time. Corinth was a commercial city located at a crossroads for travelers and traders, so its culture was cosmopolitan and very mixed. As for religion, there were twelve temples dedicated to the worship of Greek gods and goddesses in Corinth. In the worship of Aphrodite, goddess of love, who paralleled Venus from Roman mythology, temple prostitution was part of religious devotion. The Christian life and faith stood in marked contrast to the ways of most Corinthians and required Christians to make significant changes not only in belief, but in practice.

No instruction manual

First Corinthians is one of oldest writings in the New Testament after 1 Thessalonians. It circulated some years before the Gospels and is very thin on the sayings of Jesus. Corinthians of that time would not have been as familiar with the teachings of Jesus as we are and would have relied on Paul rather than on hard and fast teachings to interpret life in the new age. The Christians of Corinth are far more the products of cosmopolitan Corinth at this point than they are the products of Christian culture. But they're learning

Asceticism is the belief that there is a clear distinction between the spiritual and the physical. Furthermore, the spiritual is considered more worthy and pure. That which pertains to the physical human body or the earth is less pure, even tainted. Ascetic beliefs and practices were common in ancient Mediterranean culture, including the practice of virginity for those set apart for service to the gods and goddesses in some popular Greek cults. The first call on everyone's life, married or single, is to follow Jesus Christ. Everyone shares the same primary calling, but we live out that calling in a variety of circumstances.

—Shirley Yoder Brubaker, "One is a whole number: A Mennonite pastor presents a theology of singleness," the Mennonite, May 26, 1998.

Paul's teaching, therefore, is not strictly from the Gospels. In fact, he departs from even the Jewish teaching on marriage and tolerates remarriage after divorce, whereas Jesus taught that marriage after divorce is adultery (Matt. 5; Luke 16).

How can Paul say, seemingly against Jesus' teaching, that we can divorce if we must and remarry if we are full of passion? Paul and the young church lived in a new age that was ushered in by Jesus' death and resurrection. In a short time, Christians believed, the new age would be complete. In a short time they would not have to live a dual life in both the old age and the new age, but for the time being, Paul says, they must live new lives in an old world.

Here is the age-old question for Christians. How do we live in the world without being people of the world? We do it by choosing one reality over the other. Paul would say that when we live according to the reality of the new age, the conditions of the old world, such as marriage, slavery, and race, cannot define us as people of God. They are mere conditions of the physical world that Christ overcomes. So while we are certainly men and women, Jew and Greek, slave and free in the physical world, we meet God as new people, as people of the covenant, unfettered by old definitions.

> While Paul may have counseled sexual abstinence, Hebrew scripture includes the unabashed love poem Song of Solomon.
> *Ah, you are beautiful, my love,*
> * ah, you are beautiful;*
> * your eyes are doves.*
> *Ah, you are beautiful, my beloved,*
> * truly lovely.*
> *Our couch is green...*

Paul is not saying that because the Corinthians are Christians they are home free and may live as they please. Rather, he cautions them against believing that anything about the physical world has changed. We cannot perfect or change the givens of life. What is changed is in a different realm, a realm of the future that is present now. While we cannot change who we are in the old world, we must accept that we are changed in Christ. And the one who is changed in Christ will live in a new way, seeking reconciliation with a spouse rather than giving up on marriage. Living in the new age, does not, for Paul, mean being liberated from physical slavery, for we are liberated in Christ. And in terms of race, Gentiles should not try to become Jews or vice versa, because there are no such distinctions in the new realm in which they live.

While many Christians suffer abusive spouses, cruel masters, and racist countrymen, and would be better off if the world would change, they are surely liberated in God's eyes. What good is it, we ask, when someone is battered, enslaved, or degraded? How is religion any help at all? As Paul knew from his own experience of persecution, the power of our true identity in Christ is the true life force for us. It is this reality that gives us our ultimate value and our self-worth as people, even when others won't give it to us.

We can never erase a relationship with a former spouse, a master, or an abuser even if we start fresh and regain our physical psychological health. That old reality is part of who we are forever and ever. That is the condition Paul wants us to accept when he says, "In whatever condition you were called, brothers and sisters, there remain with God" (1 Cor. 7:24), for in remaining with God our new identity surpasses the old.

The new reality Paul wants us to accept is the reality of new life in Christ. In a quote that is often attributed to Nelson Mandela but actually written by the writer Mary Ann Williamson, our identity is not defined by the world, but by our relationship to God. She says, "Our deepest fear is not that we are inadequate. Our deepest fear is that we are powerful beyond measure. It is our light, not our darkness, that most frightens us. We ask ourselves, who am I to be brilliant, gorgeous, talented and fabulous? Actually, who are you not to be? You are a child of God."

Things to think about: Reflect this week on your principle identity. Are you primarily a parent? a divorced person? a wage-earner? spouse? friend? Christian? artist? committee member? victim? Ask yourself how others see you. Then think about how Christ sees you. Which image of yourself is best? What can you change about your life so that you are living as the person Christ knows?

PART II: SESSION

Focus (10 MINUTES)
Open the session with announcements and sharing as you usually do. Then choose an activity to focus on the topic.

Option A: As a whole group, name five or six changes that need to be made in the world. Then as individuals, imagine that you have just learned that the world will end in one year. Prioritize these changes on a slip of paper, from most urgent to least urgent, considering what you know about the end of the world. Share your priority slip with two or three neighbors or the whole group. What's worth changing in a year? Why?

Transition: Paul and the young Christian church believed that Christ would return soon. Their belief in Christ's return colored everything that they did and believed. Study 1 Corinthians 7:1-24 to see Paul's advice on living in the "in between times."

Option B: Quickly make a list of the "givens" in your life. That is, list the conditions of your life right now. Are you married? single? divorced?

middle class, rich, or poor? educated? a veteran? retired? a parent? other?
With one or two partners, talk about the effect of these givens on your
life from now on. Are you able to forget the past and go on, or do you
tend to carry your past with you in all you do?

Transition: Paul says our efforts to change the past are futile. No matter
how hard we try to change our relationships, our race or culture, and our
past enslavements, we cannot remove them as part of our lives. Real
change comes from God. 1 Corinthians 7:1-24 teaches that God changes us
from a mere classification of gender, slavery, or race to be children of God.

Engage the Text (20 MINUTES)

Option A: Divide into three groups by choice. Those who want to look
at Paul's passage on marriage and divorce (7:1-16) will meet together.
Those who want to look at his passage on circumcision (a code word for
race or culture, 7:17-20) will meet together. And those who want to look
at his discussion about slavery (7:21-24) will meet together.

In each group, listen as a volunteer reads the passage. Then examine your
passage for the difference between how the world defines who we are in
terms of marriage, race, or slavery and how God defines who we are.

Option B: Look at the issue of marriage and divorce. Listen as a volunteer reads 1 Corinthians 7:1-16 aloud. Then divide into three groups,
counting off by threes. The first group will look at 7:1-7; the second
group 7:8-11; and the third group 7:12-16. Discuss the following questions about your passage:
1. How do you think people of the world (the old age) viewed the marital
   status in the passage?
2. How does Paul want Christians (people of the new age) to view the
   marital status in the passage?
3. Does it matter to Paul whether the relationship is solid and healthy?
   Why or why not?
4. What effect does Christ coming again have on Paul's teaching in this
   passage?

Come back together as a group. Share insights about each question from
the small group discussion. Also evaluate Paul's teaching.

Option C: Compare 1 Corinthians 7:1-16 with Jesus' teaching on marriage and divorce in Mark 10:2-12. How are the teachings the same?

different? How do you account for the difference? Divide into two groups, one to spell out rules on divorce and marriage for Jesus and one to spell out rules on divorce and marriage according to this passage from Paul's writings. Talk about which set of rules we should use as the church. Why?

Respond (15 MINUTES)

Option A: Out of the "givens" listed below, share you hopes for change or your despair.

war
poverty
hatred
greed
degradation of the environment
violence

How does God see the people who the world defines mainly by these givens—the poor, the war-like, the hateful, the greedy, materialists, the violent? Strategize about how you could help these people recognize their identity as the whole people of God.

Option B: Decide whether as new people in Christ we should endure the givens of the world or work for change.

Option C: Give a "testimony" about how you live according to the "new age" and at the same time live in the world.

Closing (5 MINUTES)

Sing a song of freedom in Christ, such as "Oh freedom" or "Freedom is coming."

PART III: LEADER GUIDELINES

Items Needed

Pens and paper
Bibles
Songbooks

Session 3

Singleness: A Prophetic Option

PART I: PREPARATION

Bible passage: 1 Corinthians 7:25-40

Key verse: I want you to be free from anxieties (1 Cor. 7:32a).

Summary: Paul believed that the present age was quickly passing away. He therefore encourages Christians in Corinth to shift their lives from the old way of doing things to a new way. One of the questions Corinthians ask Paul about life in a new age is whether they should enter into marriage. Paul has already talked to them about sexual relations in the new age. Here he talks about the actual contract of marriage, which is a convention of the present age. Remaining single is not the issue. The issue is whether to live by the old conventions governed by law or to live by new covenants under Christ's reign. Paul appears to favor singleness because marriage involves responsibilities and anxieties that take time and energy away from the task of living fully in the new age. But Paul's greatest concern is that we base relationships on covenant, not the force of law. The present age is still passing away. Marriage is still a legal as well as a religious covenant in our culture. As Christians do we need legal protections in our relationships? What makes a relationship binding in a religious sense? Is celibacy the answer to avoiding a marriage contract?

Study

Last time, using the examples of divorce and remarriage, Paul talked about our identity in Christ as opposed to our identity in the present age. No matter how we change our sexual relationships, he said, we are ultimately complete, not in a partner, but in Christ. So do what is best for you, but remember that your ultimate identity is tied up in Christ. In Christ you are free, no matter how entrapped you are in the present age. In Christ you are neither male nor female, Greek nor Jew, even if that's who you are in the present age. No matter how you change your life in the present age, it does not change your life in Christ, so don't bother.

In the next passage of scripture, we continue to hear one side of the conversation between Paul and the Corinthian Christians. Beginning in 1 Corinthians 7:25, Paul responds to another issue raised by the church. They want to know, given Paul's teaching about the end of the present age, what Paul advises about both marriage and singleness. Members of the Corinthian church were apparently under the impression that Christians must convert the present age to the reign of God, which they believed called for abstinence from physical pleasures, sex, and marriage. Some went so far as to advocate divorce to free themselves for mission. But Paul quickly and boldly upheld the goodness and value of sexual fulfillment in marriage. We cannot change the present age by saintly behavior because, no matter what, the present age still depends on law instead of grace.

As young adults wait longer to marry and with half of all marriages ending in divorce, the church includes an increasing number of single adults. According to Paul's logic, this makes available a tremendous amount of time and energy for the work of the church.

In Paul's opinion, whether to marry or remain single is not a matter of moral right or wrong. He says it would be okay to do either. However, the marriage contract is a convention of the present age, and marriage is upheld by the force of law, not a covenant or commitment. So Paul voices a preference for singleness under the circumstances. In the decline of the present age, which he calls an "impending crisis" in verse 26, Paul advises remaining single. Paul believes that the present order of things will soon be changed, and people will live under Christ and not under the powers of the old way. Single people have an advantage because they will be able to devote undivided time and energy to the work of the church as it take on new life in a new age, operating according to new criteria.

Throughout much of the history of the Christian church, interpreters of this Bible passage believed Paul had a low view of marriage. They even supported the view that sex defiles those who desire the highest state of spirituality. In reality, Paul is disputing such beliefs. He makes it clear that both marriage and singleness are acceptable choices for believers.

And he does not apologize for suggesting that people remain in whatever state they were when they first converted to the Christian faith. But Paul also makes it clear that one's primary identity lies in one's relationship to Christ, not in one's marital status. The church includes all kinds of individuals—married, never married, widowed, and divorced. Nowhere does Paul say that one's standing in the community of faith is altered because of one's marital status. Marital status is not equated with emotional or spiritual maturity or with the ability to be a leader within the group.

While Paul states a clear preference for maintaining the marital status at the time of conversion, his words do not constitute dogmatic regulations for the ordering of social relationships in the Christian church. Paul leaves much to the discernment of individuals and the local community of believers. His advice to remain single comes from a belief that the old way was rapidly disappearing and Jesus Christ had ushered in the new age with his death and resurrection. The new age is not fully arrived, but it is in the process of becoming. Did Paul anticipate there would be no passion or marriage in this new age? No. But he was determined that relationships in this time between the old way and Christ's second coming would not be based on legal contracts. As long as the force of law dictates what marriage is, it is better to be single. Let love be expressed in a covenant, not a business contract that could be bought with a bride price.

> "A woman without a man is like a fish without a bicycle." We may chuckle when we see such slogans on bumper stickers or t-shirts. But we must be sure our affirmation of the single life does not degenerate into denigration of either gender or the value of marriage.

Marriage is Paul's metaphor in these chapters to distinguish between law and grace, the old way and the new way. In 1 Corinthians 7:29-31, he uses other examples of life in the new way. "The appointed time has grown short," he says. If you are married, think of yourself as single. If you're mourning the dead, don't bother because death is no longer permanent in the new age. If you're rejoicing over marriage in the present age, stop rejoicing over love reduced to laws. As for material possessions, begin to think of yourself as having nothing, of being free from encumbrances. If you're a successful business person, begin to live without contracts, rules, and regulations. "For the present form of this world is passing away" (7:31).

Marriage is a good example for Paul's teaching on the difference between the old and the new way, because in the present age, marriage requires a law to govern something that only God can sanction. But marriage is just one convention of the old way. There are many old ways. Our job as Christians is to begin to distinguish between the old and new in everything we do—in marriage, paying taxes, citizenship, parenting, and education, to name a few. The sooner we learn to make the distinction, the sooner the old age will pass away. We are the only thing that keeps the new age from happening, a burden Paul did not want to shoulder.

Things to think about: Talk with your family, friends, or co-workers this week about how you could begin to live in the new age. Here are three minor considerations. How willing would you be to make your largest charitable gift of the year without taking a tax deduction? How willing would you be to leave the church doors unlocked during the week? If you were in an accident with an undocumented immigrant, how willing would you be to pay for the damages instead of going to the police, who might arrest the immigrant?

Ten questions to ask a single person other than, "So, is there anyone special in your life?":
1. How did you like the service today?
2. How's work/school going?
3. So, what special projects are you up to these days?
4. Have you seen/read anything interesting lately?
5. How is your family doing?
6. Do you have any travel plans?
7. What do you make of [some current event]?
8. Tell me about your week.
9. What are your plans for today?
10. We'd like to have lunch with you. Could we do that? What restaurant do you recommend? Or, Do you know how to get to our house?

—Marianne Martin, the Mennonite, May 26, 1998.

PART II: SESSION

Focus (10 MINUTES)
Begin with announcements and sharing. Then choose one of the following options to focus on the session.

Option A: Divide into groups of threes. In each small group, have two people engage in conversation. The third person should try to break into the conversation while the pair tries to continue their conversation and keep out the third person. After a couple of minutes, stop and talk in the larger group. How did it feel to keep talking and ignore someone who was trying to get into the conversation? How did it feel to be the one who was left out?

Discuss how this exercise compares to the church. What kinds of people may sometimes feel like the third person in this exercise? What things about church life give messages about who is included and who is excluded? List your ideas on the blackboard or newsprint, for example: a bulletin announcement that reads "each *family* bring one hot dish to the fellowship meal" (this might make single persons wonder if they qualify as a family); publicity for an annual Valentine's Day dinner with prices at $20 for couples and $12 for singles (this may seem to singles that they are penalized for not being part of a couple); a singles group whose activities usually feature roller-skating and water skiing (which may not feel welcoming to a 75-year-old newly widowed person). Add others to the list.

Engage the Text (15 MINUTES)

Read today's passage aloud from a contemporary translation; review the background information presented in the Study section above.

Do a brainstorming exercise to identify contemporary sources and specific beliefs and practices that influence our decisions about relationships and sexual activity. For example, sources of influence might be television sitcoms and movies; specific beliefs and practices might include the expectation that casual sex is a normal part of dating. To brainstorm, individually write your ideas on sheets of paper. After a couple of minutes, pair up with one other person and combine your lists. Then gather in groups of four and combine your lists again. Finally, make one list for the entire class. (If your class is quite small, you will want to skip some of the groupings; for example, go directly from individual lists to one list for the entire group.)

For each pair in the group, select one of the items from your list. Then attempt to write a response to this item as Paul might have responded to this influence or belief. Based on the kind of advice Paul gave to the Corinthians, how do you think he would have advised today's single Christians? Would he advise remaining single? If so, on what basis? Would he advise celibacy? If so, on what basis? Would Paul offer "rules,"

A few quick comebacks for those who are trying to deflect unwanted inquiries: How's your love life? Yes, I do love life. In fact, this week I... Are you dating anyone? Yes, I manage to date myself every time I mention what television shows I watched as a kid. Do you remember the episode where...

Are you seeing anyone? No, I'm not hearing voices either; are you?

How's it going with you and so-and-so? I was wondering the same thing about you and your spouse. You go first. When are you getting married? June 32nd. Money gifts will be appreciated. Send them to my address anytime between now and then.

So, is there anyone special in your life? Yes, there are many special people in my life, and you're one of them.

—Marianne Martin, *the Mennonite,* May 26, 1998.

or would he make suggestions that leave room for some discernment by individuals or the community of faith?

Respond (15 MINUTES)

Option A: Return to the list you developed in the Focus activity. Based on the first list, create a second list of ways your congregation might be a more welcoming church family for single people. Pick at least one concrete thing you will do as a class and decide how you will implement your idea in the next week. At the beginning of next week's class, start by reporting whether this assignment has been completed.

Option B: Draw a line down the middle of a blackboard or newsprint. Using the technique of brainstorming (quickly calling out all ideas that come to mind and recording them on a blackboard or newsprint without evaluation or response), on one side list stereotypes about single adults and their involvement in church life. On the other side of the blackboard or newsprint, jot down ways the stereotypes are true or false. Are there negative notions about singleness that you can agree are completely false? If so, cross them off the list. Are there positive notions about singleness that you can agree are mostly true? If so, circle them. Ask students to share any stories from personal experience in which stereotypes were challenged or changed regarding singles in the life of the church. Who are positive role models?

> The first call on everyone's life, married or single, is to follow Jesus Christ. Everyone shares the same primary calling, but we live out that calling in a variety of circumstances.
>
> —Shirley Yoder Brubaker, "One is a whole number: A Mennonite pastor presents a theology of singleness," the Mennonite, May 26, 1998.

Closing (10 MINUTES)

Gather in the same groups of three that took part in the very first exercise in which two people conversed and tried to keep out the third. Join hands in your groups while someone reads the text of "How good a thing it is" (*Hymnal: A Worship Book* #310).

PART III: LEADER GUIDELINES

Items Needed

Newsprint and markers
Bibles
Hymnals

Tips for Leading

1. Be very sensitive that today's activities and conversations are not condescending to single people in your class or even in the congregation in general. Sometimes single people feel they are treated as if they are less mature than married people of the same age, as if being married automatically increases one's maturity. If you are single, consider sharing honestly from your own experience what it is like to be part of your church. Be prepared to especially invite the singles in your class to share their experiences, and do not let the married people dominate the discussion. If your class is made up of only married persons, you might want to consider joining with another class for this session or invite some single people in the church to join your class as special guests for the day and to speak of the joys and problems of being single in the church. In the Respond/Act section, when the class selects a way to make your church more welcoming to single people, pay special attention to hearing the wisdom of the single people who are present.

2. Check out a Mennonite pastor's theology of singleness by Shirley Yoder Brubaker, "One is a whole number," *the Mennonite*, May 26, 1998.

Session 4

Forgive and Forgive

■

PART I: PREPARATION

Bible passage: 2 Corinthians 2:2-11; 5:16-21

Key verses: If I cause you pain, who is there to make me glad but the one whom I have pained? (2 Cor. 2:2).

In Christ God was reconciling the world to himself, not counting their trespasses against them, and entrusting the message of reconciliation to us (2 Cor. 5:19).

Summary: In the first passage from 2 Corinthians, Paul alludes to an ugly encounter he had with a member of the Corinthian congregation on his last visit. Apparently the person who wronged him has now been sufficiently disciplined and should be forgiven. There is no joy in ongoing conflict, besides, as Paul says in chapter 5, the most important work of the church is reconciliation, bringing the alienated back to God. Often we do well at church discipline, but we fail at forgiveness and reconciliation. What is enough discipline? How do we joyfully welcome back the person with whom we've had serious conflict?

Study

There was trouble in Corinth...again. Like 1 Corinthians, the second letter spends a great deal of time responding to concerns and conflicts in the congregations of Corinth. In fact, the first nine chapters of 2 Corinthians are devoted to exposition on various problems, including the presence in the church of people who are undermining the leadership and authority of Paul as a spiritual guide and overseer of the fledgling Christian community. He sent his assistants Timothy and Titus on different occasions to teach and mediate, but apparently there is still reason for Paul to address the problems in Corinth.

Full restoration of community is not a simple or easy process. Carolyn Holderread Heggen writes in *Sexual Abuse in Christian Homes and Churches*, "Victims and offenders should be encouraged to work toward restored relationship. But reconciliation must be seen in the context of a longer, often difficult process which involves repentance, restitution, forgiveness—then reconciliation" (123).

Bible scholars have tried looking at 2 Corinthians in different ways—as two letters conjoined, as five letters sewn together, as two parts in reverse order, or, for lack of anything better, the letter just as we have it. Taken just as it is, curious problems jump up from the text right away. Paul says he doesn't want to make "another painful visit" (2:1), implying there was a first painful visit. In 2:4 he mentions a previous letter on this problem that we don't seem to have in either 1 or 2 Corinthians. In the end we have to live without the information.

Nowhere in Paul's writings are the details of the conflict in 2:2-11 specifically described, though we get a little more detail from 7:12. We don't learn about the conflict, but we learn that what pained Paul most was that the congregation did not come quickly to his defense. It was finally his letter mentioned in 2:4, written through anguish and tears, that finally prompted the congregation, as Titus reports in 7:7, to take disciplinary action and defend Paul.

It's not that Paul has such tender feelings or such a big ego that he personally needs to be avenged. This affront is an affront to the congregation. "But if anyone has caused pain, he has caused it not to me, but to some extent—not to exaggerate it—to all of you" (2:5). In defense of the faith, not Paul, the Corinthian congregation is finally moved to confront the offender, who in turn becomes penitent and cooperative. Some members of the community seem to think further action should be taken. But Paul suggests it is time for grace and restoration.

What is enough?

We do not know exactly how the offender exhibited sufficient penance and cooperation to allow Paul to come to the conclusion that it was time to move on. Surely Paul knew it was risky to prematurely restore the offender to congregational life, and perhaps even to a role of leadership. But Paul was adamant that confrontation and discipline in the church, while necessary, was only for the purpose of confession of sin and restoration of right relationship. Making the conditions for confession and restoration too harsh would only discourage an offender who was truly repentant.

How do we know the dividing line between sufficient disipline and "excessive" discipline (2:7)? Repentance is the key. When the offender repents and is ready to change, the congregation must shift to reconciliation so the person is not dunned with too much sorrow. But the church has gone beyond sufficiency in many cases. When the church uses excommunication, banning, castigation, confession, and, in extreme cases, death to discipline members, it has sometimes failed the test of sufficiency. Repentance cannot be the only criteria, because repentance does not satisfy some. Words can be false. A confession can easily be forced and disingenuous. Perhaps it is the motive of the disciplinarian rather than the change in the offender that determines when there has been enough discipline. And the motivation must be, according to the teaching of Paul, to restore the person to the community and to God. Use only so much discipline as you need to bring about a reconciliation.

Ministry of Reconciliation

All of Paul's exposition on problems, transgressions, unfaithfulness, and idolatry are balanced by the charge he has for us to be ministers of reconciliation. In 2 Corinthians 5:16-21, Paul explains the basis for the practice of forgiveness and reconciliation in human relationships. Paul begins in verses 16 and 17 by claiming that Christian faith changes our perspective. We see ourselves and others in new ways. We now even see Jesus differently. All who believe in Christ are literally new creatures. Here he is coming back to that common refrain of new life in Christ. Having thrown our lot in with the new age under Christ, things are going to be different. Where the present age may work on the basis of tit for tat and an eye for an eye, the ultimate goal of the new age is reconciliation and restoration.

> Then Peter came and said to him, "Lord, if another member of the church sins against me, how often should I forgive? As many as seven times? Jesus said to him, "Not seven times, but, I tell you, seventy-seven times" (Matt. 18:21-22).

Starting in verse 18, Paul explains why all things are new. It is because we have been estranged from God, but in Jesus, we are brought back into right relationship with God. Verse 20 is a powerful statement of our mission as believers in Jesus who, through him, are now reconciled to God. Our mission, is to be agents of God in modeling and extending reconciliation to others, bringing the alienated into the community of faith and into right relationship with God. This is God's ultimate purpose. And the ministry of reconciliation is our part in that ultimate purpose.

We might be tempted to think church conflict and confrontation are contemporary problems. But we see in these passages that the earliest groups of Christian believers wrestled with them also. From its beginning, the church has had to figure out what to do when the authority of leaders is undermined, when different or even dangerous beliefs are presented in the faith community, when sin is present, and how to maintain unity in the midst of sin, conflict, and diversity.

There is ample evidence in the New Testament that the early church faced many situations that threatened its unity and tranquility. For example, one of the first threats came over disagreement regarding circumcision. The first followers of Jesus were followers of the Jewish faith. When they acknowledged Jesus as Lord, they continued to practice some of the rituals of Judaism. As the gospel was shared, people who were not Jewish began to also believe and follow the teachings of Jesus. Some of the Jewish believers felt these Gentile converts must adhere to Jewish laws, including circumcision as a sign of being part of God's covenant people. Other leaders believed that requiring these ritual observances was unnecessary for Christian faith. Acts 15 records the development and resolution of this conflict.

The early church and its leaders, including Paul, were not afraid to confront sin and conflict. But the goal of such confrontation was always to restore relationships and to extend forgiveness and reconciliation. Christians are human. Even the personal relationships of the people closest to Jesus in the early church were sometimes marked by personal disagreements and separation (see the story of Paul and Barnabas parting company in Acts 15:36-41), but the church at its best has tried to model the reconciling, forgiving love of God. Being a place of grace was not easy then. It is not easy now.

Things to think about: The discipline of children in a family can be a model for the kind of discipline Paul was talking about. The goal of disciplining a child is not to avenge a wrong but to guide a child and restore him or her to a relationship with the family. Check signals with others. How did they know that their parent's discipline was conciliatory and not vengeful? Or, if discipline didn't seem conciliatory, what was the purpose of discipline in their families?

Another use of discipline in society is the prison system. What would you say is the goal of prison sentencing in our society? To make convicts pay a debt to society? To reform the convicted? Other?

Part II: Session

Focus (10 MINUTES)

Open with sharing and announcements. Then choose one of the following options to focus on the issues in the session.

Option A: Give time outs. Place an empty chair in your circle and call it the "time-out chair." Take turns drawing slips of paper from an envelope or hat with the following church infractions on them:

Taking the Lord's name in vain
Embezzling the offering
Youth group advisor serving alcohol to youth at a weekend church retreat
Gambling at a casino with the offering
Stealing electronic equipment from the church
Committing a marital infidelity with someone in the congregation
Over spending the church budget
Duplicating copyrighted material for worship without permission
Deserting a spouse and young children
Murder

When it is your turn, move to the time-out chair and decide with the group how long a person should be banished from the church for the infraction you drew.

Transition: Paul trained the church to discipline members of the congregation and hold them accountable to the faith community for wrong doing. Then he had to teach them when to stop disciplining. In 2 Corinthians Paul teaches both *when* to discipline and *how much* discipline is enough.

Option B: Make a church penal code. Use the list in Option A and decide what a just punishment would be for each infraction.

Transition: Paul had his hands full disciplining the fledgling churches under his supervision. In each case, however, his goal was to help individuals and congregations grow in faith and discipleship. Read in 2 Corinthians to see how he uses discipline to instruct and restore people.

Engage the Text (20 MINUTES)

Option A: Take a few minutes to read 2 Corinthians 2:2-11 to yourself.

Then listen as a volunteer reads the passage. Choose a "jury" of peers (four to six people) to decide how much discipline is needed to punish someone who undermines church leaders. Those in the larger group may offer suggestions for discipline and may try to persuade jurors to vote a particular way. When the group has proposed and argued for several disciplinary actions, let the jurors go into session to decide the defendant's fate.

Come back together and start the process over, but this time read 2 Corinthians 5:16-21. Make suggestions to the jury that will not only discipline but restore the offender to the congregation. When the group has proposed several restorative actions, let the jurors go into session to decide the defendant's fate.

Debrief. Look at how the two decisions of the jury differ. How does discipline change when reconciliation is the goal?

Option B: Listen as volunteers read 2 Corinthians 2:2-11 and 5:16-21. Using a pencil or marker, work through the passages, highlighting verses that reflect Paul's teaching about the present age and the new age. What phrases and sentences indicate that he is speaking about life according to the resurrected Christ and not the world as Corinthians have known it? When everyone is through, compare your markings. Highlight any passages you missed. Then discuss how we should arbitrate conflict as people in the age of the resurrected Christ.

Option C: Compare 2 Corinthians 2:2-11 and 5:16-21 to Matthew 18:15-35. Note that the gospel teaching on discipline is followed by a teaching on forgiveness. Try your hand at making a parable about forgiveness out of the situation in 2 Corinthians.

Respond (15 MINUTES)

Option A: Talk about why it's easy to discipline offenders and difficult to reconcile people both in their personal relationships and in church divisions. Use the following questions to get started.

1. Who in your congregation is equipped to handle conflicts? The pastor? Deacons? Stephen ministers? The church board?
2. What system do you have in place to formalize a reconciliation?
3. How do you know that someone has repented and should return to the community?
4. When someone has committed an offense, is your impulse to punish him or her? Why?

5. Are there offenses, such as murder or child abuse, for which someone can never be restored to the congregation or to God? Why? What, if any, are the unforgivable offenses?

Option B: Talk about whether Paul's method of discipline and reconciliation is useful outside the church. Does it work in families? In friendships? At work? Why or why not? Share instances in which you have seen it work and where it hasn't. Do not share any confidences.

Option C: Identify a relationship you have that has been broken by some kind of misunderstanding or pain. Write a letter to this person. Pour out your feelings honestly. If you did anything to cause pain in the relationship, admit it. If you have been feeling pain but never explained why you withdrew from the relationship, explain what has been happening. Try to identify what you desire for the relationship and what needs to happen for that to occur. Try to write without censoring your thoughts or feelings. When you're finished, put the letter aside. In a day or two, return to the letter. Decide whether to rewrite it. Decide whether to send it or keep it or throw it away. Whatever you do with the letter, find a way to reach out and attempt reconciliation. If you choose, share your letter with the class or describe the situation and your commitment to seek reconciliation.

Closing (5 MINUTES)

Close by singing together "Amazing grace." If you have a saxophonist in your group, include instrumental introduction and interlude. Encourage improvisation and let the song both roll up from and reach down to your innermost being.

PART III: LEADER GUIDELINES

Items Needed
Slips of paper
Hat or large envelope
Bibles
Newsprint and markers

Tips for Leading
1. Be aware of people in the group who may have experiences that are extremely difficult to forgive or whose pain is very fresh. Be prepared to assure them that forgiveness is not something that must happen on a par-

ticular time table. At the same time, there may be others who seem to revel in hanging onto past hurts. Be prepared to gently invite them to take steps toward forgiveness. Sometimes the best way to do this is to tell a story about how the inability to forgive has caused unnecessary pain and stymied growth in the one who is unable or unwilling to forgive.

2. Ahead of time print on slips of paper the offenses listed in the Focus activity.

3. Make use of Bible dictionaries, commentaries, and concordances. Encourage people to look up terms they're unfamiliar with and use Bible encyclopedias to read about Bible times and practices mentioned in the text.

4. Be prepared to moderate activities such as the jury deliberations. Be a timekeeper and keep discussion and action moving. Know when to allow good discussion to continue and when to abandon a discussion that is going nowhere.

Session 5

The Body of Christ: Each Part Different, Each Part Necessary

■

PART I: PREPARATION

Bible passage: 1 Corinthians 12:12-31

Key verse: For just as the body is one and has many members, so it is with Christ (1 Cor. 12:12).

Summary: Paul uses the analogy of the human body to describe the community of faith. His eloquent word picture paints the church as a place where the gifts of every person are welcome and equally acceptable. Just as the human body contains many different parts having different, but necessary, functions, so is the church made up of many people having different, but necessary, gifts. While only a few are personally endowed with great talents, the gift of the Spirit comes to each. As equals in the Spirit, striving for position is futile. Still, the church today often functions like a corporation, rewarding the gifted and powerful more than others. Realistically, how can we make unity out of diversity? How can we truly appreciate the gifts and abilities of all? Why do we pay professional ministers in the church when we preach that everyone's ministry is important?

Study

A few members of a Corinthian congregation were flaunting their ability to speak in tongues, that is, to speak spontaneously in languages they had never studied. Sometimes these utterances went without translation and people were claiming divine inspiration that came only to them. Worship was becoming a circus. Furthermore, envy and arrogance about the seeming importance of this ability was causing friction and disunity among believers. Paul's primary concern, as in every passage we've looked at in this study, is to persuade Corinthian Christians to abandon the mode of operation of the world, which is passing away, and adopt the new way under Christ, a way of unity and mutuality.

> When a choir or congregation sings in harmony, all parts are needed. No one is indispensable. Even when the melody is lovely, often the most beautiful music is created when there is harmony. Whether there are one or more lines of harmony, the most full sound happens when all the voices are heard.

Paul's description of the church as a body is part of a longer passage that encompasses chapters 12–14. In chapter 12 Paul teaches about spiritual gifts and the need for unity in the church. Chapter 13 describes the greatest spiritual gift, love, and proclaims that it is available to all believers, not just those who claim a direct connection to God. And finally in chapter 14 Paul returns to the issue of worship and applies his teachings to their problem.

The body was used as another metaphor in Paul's day. We've seen it used in the Bible to refer to family structures, for instance. The man is the head of the wife. The parents are the head of the family, and the children are below them. Slaves are last of all. Religious folks used the body to illustrate a hierarchy among the faithful. Those closest to God were at the head. Those with the least access to God were at the foot of the body. But Paul shakes things up by noting that the body is a bad image for hierarchy because all of its parts are necessary to it and cannot be listed in order of greatest to least. You might be able to take away a foot or a hand, but if we take away too many parts, the body soon loses its shape. It is no longer a body. For a body to be a body, it must have the elemental parts in it.

All along in 1 and 2 Corinthians, Paul has been training the church to give up on the present age and step into the age of the resurrected Christ where everything is different. Everything operates out of a different mode. The church must operate as a machine like the body, not as a caste system with elites at the top and the untouchables at the bottom. A hierarchy is the way that is operative in the present age that is passing away.

Already we have seen Paul apply the same teaching on the new age to sexual relationships and to the life of the unmarried. Now he is asking that the church view worship from a new point of view. This new point of view, however, is not a view from beyond our messy reality. Paul never advocates severing ourselves from the physical world or denying that it exists. He counsels us to live fully in this world (as slaves, as Jews, as the divorced, the married, the unmarried, as male, as female), but we are to live as if the reign of Christ is upon us. Now a body is surely a thing of this world. It is the perfect image for existing in the here and now *and* the perfect image for operating in a new way, as a diverse unity, as a whole made up of equally valuable parts.

Paul takes another unexpected turn with this metaphor. While modern people might think of our diversity within the body as reverence for the individual, Paul thought of diversity as interdependence. Hebrews especially believed that an individual was an embodiment of the whole. No person was an "island unto himself." Whatever happened to one, affected the whole community, so a disgrace committed by a person was a disgrace to the family and to the whole community. A whole community would be judged for a murder committed by one of its members. It was not possible to single out an individual without acknowledging his or her connection to the whole community. In the same way, our congregations are not simply a collection of individuals, but a network or organism of parts. What affects one affects the whole.

What was all the fuss about at Corinth anyway? Apparently there was disagreement about how worship should be conducted. Today's church also has tensions about worship. Should we sing from a hymnal or from words flashed on a screen by an overhead projector? What translation of the Bible should be used for public reading? May women be song leaders and worship leaders? Is the gift of speaking in tongues an accepted part of the worship life of our congregation? While it is not wrong to have different opinions or to appreciate different styles of worship, perhaps Paul would still caution us today to treat one another with respect and dignity when we discuss these differences.

Instead of using the body to show that some people are better than others, Paul points out how all parts of the human body are interdependent and therefore necessary for optimal health and functioning of the entire system. But when our own bodies are in good health, we sometimes forget the truth of Paul's analogy precisely because everything works together so smoothly. Then we break an arm or a leg and we are suddenly reminded that one arm or one leg does not function as well by itself. Nor do the legs or arms generally do the same work as the other. We forget how our eyes and ears work together until we cannot see or hear well and the other organ tries to compensate for the impaired ability.

The implications for the church are powerful and clear. The health and proper functioning of the church requires the abilities and gifts of many different kinds of people. As often as some of us are overly proud of a talent for some ministry, others of us feel less capable or less important than someone else. For the good of the body, however, we must not be shy or embarrassed about offering our abilities for the ministry of the church.

I have on my table a violin string.
It is free.
But it is not free to do what a violin string is supposed to do—produce music.
So I take it, fix it in my violin and tighten it until it is taut. Only then is it free to be a violin string.

—Sir Ravindranath Tagore

In its early years together, my congregation needed a pianist to accompany congregational singing. It was a small congregation and there were not many musicians. One woman had the ability to play, but in other congregations she had always left this ministry to others whom she felt were more capable. Recognizing the need in our small group and wanting to support the worship ministry of the congregation, she finally agreed to offer her abilities. She made a commitment to practice and to play the piano according to her abilities and she made a deliberate effort not to compare herself to other pianists. Her willingness to offer her gifts because they were needed in the life of the church, even when she sometimes felt less qualified than others, has been an important element in building a meaningful worship life together as a community of faith. If she had refused, she would have been like a leg refusing to walk because it was not as strong as the legs of a trained Olympic runner. In the age of the resurrected Lord that is already upon us, we offer our gifts for the good of the whole.

Things to think about:
1. Try your hand at expanding the analogy of the body. Think of the essential ministries needed in worship. What part of the body does each represent? If you think better visually, sketch a diagram and bring it with you to the group meeting.
2. Formulate an opinion about professional paid ministry. Who should be paid for their work in the church? How much? Do you have different expectations of someone you pay than of a volunteer? Are paid ministers free to say what they feel?

Part II: Session

Focus (10 minutes)
Open with sharing and announcements. Then choose one of the following options to focus on the topic of this session.

Option A: Watch as two volunteers are blindfolded and asked to perform tasks, such as finding their way across the room to pick up an item or selecting and playing a certain CD in a stereo system. Then watch as two more volunteers are given earplugs or headphones and asked to sit in chairs placed back to back, several feet apart. Listen as the volunteers try to read alternating verses or paragraphs from a Bible or other book. While the two read, make low level noise by moving feet on the floor or talking. Finally, use handkerchiefs or a clean sock to "gag" two more volunteers. Listen as they try to tell the group what they would like to eat and drink or what they have planned for the rest of the day.

Debrief, allowing the volunteers to describe how they felt while trying to do these activities. Observers may also comment on what they saw or how the exercise reminded them of the life of the church.

Option B: Assign each class member a physical impairment. Possibilities might include being blindfolded or wearing glasses smeared with petroleum jelly, wearing earplugs or headphones, immobilizing an arm by tying it in place, using crutches with instructions to not use one leg, being confined to a wheelchair; add others as needed. More than one person can have the same handicap or some people could be given more than one handicap. When everyone has received a handicap, assign two or more teams, give instructions, and hold a brief relay race. Ask members to transport a small ball or an inflated balloon several feet forward and then back to the starting line, and pass the item to the next person.

When the race is finished, ask participants to describe how they felt while trying to do these activities.

Transition: Paul feared that like the culture around them, congregations valued some abilities and talents over others. The admiration of "beautiful people" and the neglect of people without status can leave a congregation incomplete and divided. Paul uses the complex system of the body as an analogy for how the church body should be.

Option C: Share your extended analogies from "Things to think about." Or flesh out the following analogies to illustrate interconnectedness. List all the people involved in each set. Try to determine who is most important and who should be paid the most for what they do. Talk about how the absence of one person or function in each set affects the whole. General contracting company

Surgical staff
School staff
Farm operation
Life forms and elements in a pond

Transition: All of life is interconnected, even the church. It is a collection of gifts *and* a set of gifts that are thoroughly interconnected. What is good for one is good for all. What's bad for one is bad for all. Paul faced this reality in a congregation in Corinth, and he used the analogy of the body to help Corinthian Christians see their interconnectedness.

Engage the Text (15 MINUTES)
Turn to 1 Corinthians 12 in your Bibles and read aloud verses 12 to 31.

Option A: Listen as a volunteer reads 1 Corinthians 12:12-31 aloud. This is a good passage to draw or pantomime as it's being read. On newsprint posted around the room, divide into groups and create cartoons to illustrate the passage.

Then apply the analogy to your congregation. What do the body parts represent? For instance, the music leader might be a mouth, the pastor an ear, the outreach committee a hand. Talk about the various stratifications in your congregation. Are you a body with only eyes? only ears? only hands? What are the most prized parts of the church body? Where are the hidden talents in your congregation? Where could you find the talents to complete the church body?

Option B: Make a readers theater out of this passage. Use a contemporary English translation or paraphrase 1 Corinthians 12:12-31 in your own words. If creating a paraphrase, consider metaphors for the local congregation other than the one used by Paul in this passage. Consider metaphors from your own imagination or experience. Work in groups that are small enough so you can discuss your ideas as you work. If the class is quite large, perhaps only part of the class will work on this while another group does Option A. Or work in small groups to produce several renditions of the text. Present them to each other.

Option C: Read 1 Corinthians 12:12-31 several times.
The first time: Look or listen for Paul's teaching on diversity and unity. Come to an agreement in the group about what Paul says about unity and diversity.

The second time: Look or listen for Paul's teaching on interdependence and interconnectedness. How does your congregation model good interdependence? How is the life of the pastor connected to the life of the custodian and how is the life of the board chair connected to the youth group?

The third time: Look or listen for how the church must worship in the age of the resurrected Lord as opposed to the present age that is passing away. How does your worship depart from the standards of the world and conform to life in the new age?

Respond (20 MINUTES)

Option A: With class members gathered in a circle, have members turn to the person to their left and complete the sentence "If you were not here, I would miss..." or "You bring...to our class/church." If you have plenty of time available or a very small class, each person can complete the sentence for each other person in the circle. Another option is to write these messages on note cards and present them to one another.

Option B: Sit as a group around a table. Place refreshments on the table. With kite string or yarn, loosely tie your left wrist to the right wrist of the person on your left. Tie your right wrist to the left wrist of the person on your right. When the circle is tied together, begin to eat your refreshments. Watch the kind of teamwork that develops to carry out this task. When everyone has eaten, ask members to discuss how it felt to work together in this way. What are examples of the church working together to accomplish common goals?

Closing (5 MINUTES)

Close with a prayer of thanksgiving for the gifts of each person in the room and for the church as the body of Christ. Sing together a song of unity and diversity, such as "There are many gifts" (based on today's scripture text) or "Brethren, we have met to worship" or "Heart with loving heart united."

PART III: LEADER GUIDELINES

Items Needed

Newsprint and markers
Refreshments, including something to drink
String or yarn
Bibles, including a contemporary translation

Tips for Leading

1. You will need to select specific ideas and gather materials for the exercises involving physical impairments (blindfolds, earplugs, etc.). Be sensitive to those in the group who may have physical disabilities already. If appropriate, invite them to help illustrate the lesson. Also, remember that every individual has greater and lesser abilities. In group discussion, find out what disabilities each one of us faces.

2. Pay attention to the learning styles of participants. Do most people like to discuss? Do they learn through art? drama? debate? Choose a variety of options so that everyone in the group has the opportunity to learn in the best way possible.

3. When discussing the congregation, guide the conversation away from personalities and toward talents. Avoid using this session as a gripe session.

Session 6
Dedicated Disciples Dig Deep

PART I: PREPARATION

Bible passage: 2 Corinthians 8:1-15

Key verse: For you know the generous act of our Lord Jesus Christ, that though he was rich, yet for your sakes he became poor, so that by his poverty you might become rich. (2 Corinthians 8:9)

Summary: Throughout his letters to the Corinthians, Paul teaches believers in Christ to act differently than nonbelievers. In today's passage the issue is money. The mother church in Jerusalem is struggling to make ends meet while Macedonian Christians have extra financial resources. Paul prods the Corinthians, who said in the past that they would be willing to help, to make a donation, but only if it is done in the spirit of Christ. It was Christ who gave up everything to live among us so that we would be rich beyond measure. Now we are to do the same. What is our motivation for giving to the church? Does it come out of a feeling of duty or out of grace and an impulse to share as Jesus shared?

Study

The mother church in Jerusalem has fallen on hard times. Perhaps in their zeal to sell all, give to the poor, and live like Jesus, they gave away the farm. No one knows for sure. But now the church that started it all and gave inspiration and courage to so many others is struggling. Elsewhere in the Bible Paul speaks of a fund drive to collect money for Jerusalem. Mention is made in Romans, 1 Corinthians, and Galatians. Luke mentions it in Acts. The outlying congregations are sending contributions to support the church that spawned a whole movement.

St. Francis of Assisi (d. 1226) was the son of a successful Italian merchant family. But he rejected family wealth, the business world, and a military career to live a life of poverty in order to serve the church and minister to the poor. The requirements of those who joined Francis in ministry included giving up all possessions and living a life of simplicity, poverty, and service.

In Paul's second letter to the Corinthians, Paul speaks about the collection again. He says the money is being received to assist the "saints" (elsewhere referred to as the poor) of the church in Jerusalem. The Corinthian Christians have already made a commitment to offer assistance and have made at least one contribution. Now Paul encourages them to follow through to complete their commitment and may be inviting them to be more generous than they have already been. As motivation, Paul holds up the believers in a sister congregation in Macedonia where the members are even more economically strapped than the Corinthians but have still managed to give a substantial gift. No one had to ask the Macedonians for money. They "begged" to be involved in the effort.

Paul is quick to point out in verse 5 that the Macedonians "gave themselves first to the Lord and, by the will of God, to us." Giving is something that God does through us. It is not something that we do by or for ourselves. Therefore, our gifts do not glorify us but God. The Macedonian gift, then, is an indication of their great faith and of God's gift of grace.

Paul hopes in verse 8 that the Corinthian congregations are as faithful, and he uses this comparison perhaps to incite a little competition. But in all seriousness, the real comparison is between heaven and earth. Jesus gave up everything to be incarnated on earth where he had nothing. And in human form, he gave everything so that we could be rich. The resurrection of Jesus makes it possible for his followers to share in the riches of life with God. Just as Jesus shared in the poverty of those he loved, and shared with them his riches, the Corinthian believers should share with the Jerusalem church. Generosity among the churches would help meet the needs of all. Paul does not suggest that the Corinthians should be poor. But it is not right for the Corinthians to have an abundance when their sister church has too little.

We might as well get rid of our excess. The danger of hanging onto our wealth, as Paul points out, is that we can easily lose it all. At the end of this passage, Paul refers to the Exodus story of manna from heaven (Exod. 16:18). It is by divine providence that we even have wealth in the first place. The Israelite nation was traveling through the wilderness on the way from Egypt to the Promised Land. When food was scarce in the wilderness the people complained to their leaders, who in turn prayed to God. A food called manna, a whitish substance that lay on the ground each morning, provided sustenance for the people throughout their long journey. God's specific instruction was to collect a certain portion for each person in the morning. If more food was gathered than was needed for one day, it spoiled the second day. However, they were to gather double portions on the day before the sabbath. Manna collected in preparation for the sabbath did not spoil on the second day, allowing the Israelites to observe a day of rest. When Paul refers to this story in his letter to the Corinthian Christians, he is suggesting that God continues to provide for the faithful ones. But if the needy are greedy and try to amass a fortune, the riches come to nothing. In the case of the early Christian churches, divine providence came in the form of offerings received from wealthier congregations for needy congregations. God would meet the needs of the Jerusalem church through the generosity of believers in other places, such as Corinth and Macedonia.

As we have seen in other lessons, the church today continues to experience many of the same problems as the first Christians. We also have evidence of similar faithful participation in the life of Christ's body. Many congregations invite members to pledge the amount they expect to contribute to the annual budget. Pledges allow budget makers to make realistic decisions about expenditures. One congregation was facing a budget for the next year that had been trimmed as much as possible, however anticipated income was still lower than anticipated expenses. The finance committee went back to the congregation with a copy of the budget outlining programs and ministries that were being supported. They asked the congregation to consider making additional pledges. One of the first responses was from a young couple who were students living on a limited income. Their pledge indicated they would contribute $10 more per week to the church budget. The finance committee felt humbled and grateful. A few dollars a week may not seem like much in the big picture of a church budget. But to the young couple, those few dollars out of their meager finances was a significant portion.

"People who give generously to charity are not necessarily those who can afford it," writes Tim Stafford in Christianity Today. "In fact, the weakest givers (giving the lowest proportion of their income) are those making from $40,000 to $100,000 per year. The two groups that give the highest percentages of their income to charity or church are those who make less than $20,000 a year and those who make more than $100,000."

Their pledge probably indicated a willingness to give up a movie or a lunch date. This young couple knew they were part of something bigger than themselves. They contributed as they were able. Their contribution was a valuable and necessary part of meeting the need.

Reformer John Calvin reflected the common practice of his time by suggesting that one-fourth of all church income be used to assist needy persons within the congregation, with another one-fourth used for needy persons outside the congregation. Fully one-half of a congregation's income was to be used to assist persons with financial needs.

—Larry Woiwode (interview by Harold Fickett in *Image: A Journal of the Arts and Religion*, Spring 1994)

Things to think about: Work out an informal budget for the next twelve months. Remember that you are simply the steward of God's money. Take your charitable giving off the top of your income and adjust spending elsewhere. Where could you trim your budget to make more giving possible? Strive to budget as much as possible for others. Then challenge yourself to implement the budget.

PART II: SESSION

Focus (10 MINUTES)

Open with sharing and announcements. Then choose one of the options below to focus on the theme of the session.

Option A: Amass a fortune. Choose a company from the stock report in the newspaper in which to invest $100,000 hypothetically. Make sure you choose one that no one else in the group has chosen. Check the value of the stock each day, Monday through Friday, of the previous week. How much did you gain or lose? What would you do with the surplus? Reinvest it, keep it, or give it away? Why?

Option B: Think of a time when you had a need that was met by a friend, family member, the church, or a community service agency. Now think about a time when you had an abundance of resources and helped meet someone else's needs. Turn to the person next to you and identify how you felt in each situation. In the larger group, make two lists on a blackboard or piece of newsprint—a composite list of feelings associated with being the receiver of a gift, and one composite list of feelings associated with being the giver. Is it better to give than receive or better to receive than give? Why? How are you at asking for assistance for yourself? for others?

Option C: In turn, declare yourself to be rich or poor. Then go around the circle again. If you said you were rich, what are your assets? Be sure to include assets other than monetary ones. If you think of yourself as poor, what do you lack? Money? Things? Other?

Engage the Text (20 MINUTES)

Option A: Paul is a fundraiser in this passage. Based on direct mail appeals you have received, inviting you to support many causes, make 2 Corinthians 8:1-15 into a direct mail campaign. All together, make a list of items to include in a fundraising packet, such as a letter, pictures, a small poster, and a reply card. Set about making samples of these components. If you are a large group, divide into smaller groups to accomplish the work. Use quotations from the passage in your work. When each group is finished, come back together to share your work.

To shorten this activity, read the passage aloud and then discuss how parts of it could be used for a fund drive. Would you be convinced by Paul's appeal? What makes you want to give when asked?

Option B: Using the Bible translation selected in advance (see Leader Guidelines below), class members will read the passage aloud. Then ask the class to create a "human sculpture" of the individuals or groups in this passage. Ask one or more individuals to represent each of the following: Jesus, the Jerusalem church, the Macedonian church, the Corinthian church, Titus. Tell them they must arrange themselves in still-life poses to represent the relationships and actions among the individuals or groups. For example, a person kneeling before someone standing may represent a relationship of need or inferiority. Talk to one another as you make decisions and get into position. If the class is large, divide into smaller groups to make statues.

Respond (15 MINUTES)

Option A: As a group look at copies of your church budget. Make a list on a chalkboard or newsprint of the programs and ministries you support outside of your own congregation. This will likely include things like congregational outreach ministries, local service projects, and denominational agencies. Remember to include items that may be "hidden" in another category, such as church planting or mission work that is included in a district conference or denominational budget. Try to think of special projects you support throughout the year that may be above your approved budget. How do you feel about your list? You may be pleasantly surprised to see the many ways you support the work of the church beyond your local congregation. Are you disappointed with a small list or a low percentage of your overall budget? Are there things you would like to add as a special project of your class, or take as a request to the whole congregation to be included in next year's budget?

Option B: Have mini-discussions. In groups of four or five people, talk about the following questions for two minutes each. Appoint a timekeeper.
1. Take turns naming causes in the church you would "beg" to support if you had the money.
2. What keeps you from contributing anyway?
3. Explore with each other why it is hard to part with our resources.
4. How do you feel about supporting lost causes?
5. How certain must you be that your contributions are being well spent?
6. What would it take for you to switch from giving out of your surplus to giving sacrificially?
7. What would have to change in your life in order to make sacrificial gifts?

Option C: Look through several issues of recent denominational magazines or newspapers. As a group decide on a congregation or agency in need of financial assistance and make a contribution. Take a spontaneous offering or make pledges. Then do more than send money; call the church or agency, talk to someone, hear what's happening. Or appoint someone in the group to send a letter describing your class and its desire to support their work and their needs.

Closing (5 MINUTES)
End the class with an offering. Spend a moment looking through your pockets, purse and wallet for some symbol of yourself and your resources, other than money. Pass a basket, or place your offering at the center of the meeting space. Items offered may be include such things as a date book, driver's license, mirror, car or house keys. As items are being offered, sing or listen to an offering hymn, such as "Will you let me be your servant?" or "God, whose giving." Close with a prayer of blessing and dedication.

Part III: Leader Guidelines

Items Needed

Newsprint or chalkboard
Paper and pens
Newspapers from the previous week
Examples of direct mail fundraising material
Copies of the church budget
Bibles
Denominational magazines or newspapers

Resources

Best, Ernest. *Second Corinthians* (Interpretation Series). Louisville: John
Knox Press, 1987.

Tips for Leading

1. Examine several translations of this passage ahead of time and select
   one that is easy to read and understand. Contemporary translations,
   such as *Today's English Version* (Good News Bible) and
   Contemporary English Version would be good choices. Provide Bibles
   or photocopies of the translation you have chosen.
2. Several activities require materials that you will need to collect at
   home during the week. Read through the lesson early and choose the
   activities you will use. Gather the items you will need to lead the
   activities you have chosen.
3. Money matters are very private for some people. Do not ask people to
   disclose their income or how much money they give to the church. *Do*
   urge people to think of their money as God's.